Dedicated to Trinity Joy Coulter. I have been missing your hugs, smile, and joy since September 7, 2020. I can't wait to ride horses with you in Heaven.

International Standard Book Number:
978-8-79914-694-8
Edited by Annie Oyer
Published by Jordan Daniel Chitwood

Introduction: Helping Hurting People Find Hope

My heart was not designed to carry this much grief.

On December 17, 2013, my life was shattered and ripped out from underneath me. After hearing the news that my father had passed away unexpectedly and without warning, I prematurely entered into the journey of loss without any indication that what I was feeling was normal.

Prematurely. Is there truly any age or time that it is appropriate to grieve?

At seventeen years old, it was unclear how I was supposed to feel and respond towards a loss so brutal and devastating. I learned early on that grief affects individuals differently and at different times. While some respond outwardly and appreciate company, others need space and opportunities to internally process. Some people ugly-cry while others struggle to shed a tear. Some write out their thoughts while others verbalize them to a therapist. As a seventeen-year-old, I wasn't sure how to respond towards the emotions I was feeling.

They were raw.

They felt unnatural.

They were new.

They were unlike anything I had ever felt before.

A Painful Realization

I came to the realization that loss is a part of life that nobody wants to deal with yet everyone is required to endure. Some lose a parent and are forced to journey the rest of their life without them. Others lose their child and have to face the pain of burying their own flesh. Some lose a relative and others lose their closest friend. While each loss is difficult and unique in its own way, every loss is burdensome.

No matter the age or reason for the loss, many of us begin wrestling with questions that don't have helpful answers. Questions such as:

If God is *good*, why does suffering exist?

If God is *love*, why do the good die young?

Will I *always* feel this way?

Will I *ever* get through this?

Is there *hope* at the end of this nightmare?

Where are *You*, God?

Do You *hear* me?

Do You *see* me?

Do you know *where* I am?

Where are You in the midst of my *pain*?

You're Not Alone

Whatever stage of life you find yourself in as you begin this devotional, I want you to know that these questions are not only normal, but also healthy for us to wrestle with. I think it is very natural for us as human beings to walk through seasons of doubt and discouragement. In fact, I would argue it is *unnatural* for us to act as though things are okay when we are journeying through grief and loss.

If I never allow myself to wrestle with God, am I truly willing to stand in front of Him and accept my reward? Am I truly willing to pride myself on my relationship with Jesus if it is never real and raw? A relationship with God without moments of wrestling and doubt is not a relationship at all.

There must be moments of darkness so we can appreciate His Light.

In fact, I am willing to say that we cannot truly accept the gift of love until we experience the pain and hopelessness of journeying through suffering. So wherever you are on the journey of grief and loss, I want you to feel safe here.

You are not alone.

Hope In The Mourning

I wrote this poetic devotional because I have a desire to help hurting people find hope. I have found that my pen is my arsenal in fighting the good fight while journeying through suffering. I am also at a place in my journey where I feel hope again. God has shown me His love in more ways than I can count over the years since losing my dad, and I want to help others connect to His hope through this devotional.

In the middle of my brokenness, God has appeared in so many beautifully-broken ways. God has shown me there is *Hope In The Mourning*. In the cracks of the chaos, God has bent down and picked me up, just as Christ did with Peter (see Matthew 14:31).

I firmly believe we are never alone. I believe God is close to us in our brokenness and never abandons us. This is why the Psalmist writes, "The Lord is close to the brokenhearted and saves those who are crushed in spirit" (Psalm 34:18, NIV).

This poetic journey through loss will expose the realness and rawness of the journey I have been on since 2013 to reactivate my faith and find hope in God throughout my suffering. It will expose the ugly parts of my faith—parts you have probably experienced on your journey as well. It will hold nothing back and will show you how God welcomes our authenticity.

Broken up into five parts—each part showing a different side of loss and suffering—this poetic devotional will give you an opportunity to be real with God and reflect on your own loss. Each part contains a variety of poems, prayers, excerpts, and stories to read one day at a time, with reflection questions and a Bible verse to process at the end. Nothing is off-limits. God wouldn't want it to be.

God is big enough to handle our grief in any form it comes.

My hope for you while reading through *Hope In The Mourning* is this: Allow yourself the space to be real with God. There may be poems and questions that you resonate with completely. You may read a line and think, "That is exactly how I feel/felt." You may read something and think to yourself, "I have never felt that way." That's okay. Because everyone grieves and experiences loss differently, I don't expect you to resonate with everything I have experienced.

My hope is that you connect the pain you are feeling to the God who cares for you as you journey through this devotional (see Psalm 55:22).

Lastly, this devotional is not going to cure you of your grief. After you complete this thirty-day journey, you will still experience immense pain. Each section is designed to be revisited as you experience different moments of grief throughout the *rest of your life*. Grief is not something we check off the list—it is something we will feel at different times and in different ways.

I invite you to enter into this poetic journey with an open mind and open heart—feeling comforted that someone else is journeying through something similar and has found *Hope In The Mourning*.

Part 1: Death Has Arrested

"You never know how much you really believe anything until its truth or falsehood becomes a matter of life and death to you." - C.S. Lewis, *A Grief Observed*

Day 1: My Final Day With You

What would I do if I knew, that this would be my final day with you?

Would I apologize for everything I did to you?

Would I hug you and never let go?

Would I hold your hand like when I was a kid?

What would I do if I knew, that this would be my final day with you?

Would I clean my room and fold my laundry to avoid your yell?

Would I do the dishes so you could rest?

Would I rub your feet even though they smelled?

What would I do if I knew, that this would be my final day with you?

Would I tell you how much you mean to me?

Would I tell you how proud I am to know you?

Would I share all of my dreams?

What would I do if I knew, that this would be my final day with you?

Would I ask you to hang out with me?

Would we plan a final movie night?

Would we spend the entire day talking?

What would I do if I knew, that this would be my final day with you?

Would I tell you how cool of a person you are?

Would I tell you how much you mean to me?

Would I ask you about your sins and scars?

I wonder what I would do if I knew, that this was my final day with you

Hope In The Mourning Question: What did your final day on earth with your loved one/s consist of? Even if you weren't with your loved one the day before they passed, what did you do with this person the last time you saw them? Journal below:

____

____

____

____

____

____

____

____

____

____

____

Day 2: There Are No Words

There are no words to describe a loss like this,

It's as if my heart keeps breaking again, and again, and again

Your hugs will always be missed,

Still I sit here frozen like ice

God, you're close to the broken-hearted, well here I lie

Will I ever feel hope again?

How can a good God let people die?

I wish I knew the answer

My heart was not designed to carry this much grief,

It's burning with pain each broken breath

I'm screaming out that it should have been me!

Unfortunately, God doesn't work that way

Your encouragement never ran short,

You always cared deeply for others

My heart is shattered, hear my cries, Lord.

I feel my life wasting away

I'm waiting for a cure that won't come,

Loss waits for nobody

For death is only curable by one,

I'd be foolish to continue hoping for this miracle

The thunder roars almost on cue,

As my eye forms a single tear

Life feels like a game we were destined to lose,

Is there any way to avoid this kind of grief?

I feel my strength evaporate,

Like water fleeing the grip of the desert

Maybe one day my faith will reactivate,

Right now I sit in silent pain

Hope In The Mourning Question: If you could say anything to your past self to comfort your hurting heart, what would you say? Journal below:

Day 3: The Weight of Loss

Heavier than gravity
Indescribable like the taste of water
The weight of loss buries me

Unannounced pain
Irreplaceable life
The weight of loss is unpredictable

Shaken to the core
Unstable change
The weight of loss disrupts normality

Pressured to heal
Mourning stigmas surround me
The weight of loss never goes away

Questions upon Questions
"What if's" overwhelm the soul
The weight of loss carries my hope away

Hope In The Mourning Question: After experiencing an indescribable loss, it can be difficult for us to wrap our mind around how this loss will impact our future. What are three things that have changed in your life since you lost your loved one? Journal below:

____

____

____

____

____

____

____

____

____

____

____

____

Day 4: Prayer for Understanding

Dear God, I am broken, melancholy and feeling hopeless. I am hurting while struggling to understand Your plan.

I pray that You give me the ability to understand that there are some things I will never comprehend. As I sit here with my hands shaking, I reflect on the life of my loved one. I crave the moments when we were together. I crave the conversations that were deeper than weather. I wish I could go back and soak up all of the moments I thought I'd be able to relive for many more years. I am in mourning knowing their memories are followed by tears.

Father, I don't even know what to pray. Every time I open my mouth I don't know what to say. My heart is sealed shut and refuses to seek faith. I ask that You continue showing me Your ways, wisdom, and strength every single day. Because right now, I have nothing left. I know there are things I will never fully grasp about who You are. I pray that You would begin to stretch my faith and take me farther than I am willing to go.

Open my eyes, expand my trust, and deepen my love for You. I don't want to hate You for this loss; instead, I want to grow from the pain that has been presented to me. Please expand my hope and strengthen my trust in who You say You are.

Signed, from someone who feels far, far, away from You.

Amen.

Hope In The Mourning Prayer: Write out your own "Prayer for Understanding" below.

Day 5: Where Did Everyone Go?

The day after the funeral I'd never re-live,

Where did everyone go?

My support system vanished like snow in the wake of Spring

It's as if I experienced a second fatal blow

I truly am alone

I've been forsaken

Where are You God?

My faith in You is breaking

My body is aching from every tear I cry

Who is here to wipe them away?

The grief-hype-train is over

I was a fool to think everyone would stay

So here I lay in snot-covered shirts and defeat

Where does my hope come from?

Some say You, still, I'm not so sure

I keep questioning the things You could have done

Strength? I have none

I'm never going to feel strong again

If they abandoned me, won't You, too?

When will healing begin?

I just remembered that holidays will never be the same

I feel guilty even celebrating

The only Christmas present I want is their presence

And their birthday will be devastating

My life is now a time bomb teasing detonation

Will I be the next to die?

Part of me hopes for this outcome

Yet my family needs me alive

I'm not suicidal

But I wouldn't mind dying

For if death would reunite us,

I wouldn't mind trying

Unsatisfying, horrifying, and mummifying thoughts keep haunting me

I wish I could wake from this nightmare

Where did everyone go?

I am aching for the support to reappear

Hope In The Mourning Question: What has your loss taught you about supporting others during their loss-journey? Journal below:

____

____

____

____

____

____

____

____

____

____

____

____

Day 6: Reflection Questions & Reactivate Faith Verse

1) Who have you lost in your life? Print out a picture of them and tape it below:

2) When did you lose this person?

3) How did you lose this person?

4) What are your real and raw feelings about losing this person?

5) Are you angry with God that this person is gone?

6) Are you angry with yourself that this person is gone?

Reactivate Faith Verse: *"The Lord is close to the brokenhearted and saves those who are crushed in spirit" (Psalm 34:18, NIV).*

Part 2: Good Mourning, Child

"Love knows not its own depth until the hour of separation." - Khalil Gibran

Section Introduction: Ugly Tears or Happy Tears?

If loss has taught me anything about my personality that I didn't know before, it taught me that I am an *ugly crier*. In fact, I don't know how to cry beautifully.

As I began mourning the loss of my dad, I found myself breaking down with sweaty eyes and a snotty nose at the most unexpected times. One time, while driving back from visiting my grandparents in Michigan for a few days, my heart decided to *continue healing*.

My dad's favorite worship song—10,000 Reasons—began playing on the radio. As soon as the chorus hit, I felt my knees buckle under the wheel and my eyes begin to swell up. My chest tightened while my vocal chords expressed themselves in a way that only God could understand.

Tears rolled down my puffy cheeks while snot collected at the top of my lip. In between hyperventilating and what felt like hiccup-crying, I attempted to breathe. *Ugly-crying hits at the worst times.*

Mourning

Merriam Webster's Dictionary defines mourning as an outward sign of grief for a person's death. In other terms, mourning is the *spiritual*, physically breaking through the barriers we have built up since the loss of our loved one.

While mourning is different for everyone, one thing needs to be clear: this is not a phase we go through and then never experience again. While mourning is often more common during the weeks after the death of your loved one, you will experience different types and times of mourning for the rest of your life.

Seven years after the death of my dad, I am still physically expressing the loss of him through ugly-crying and loss of appetite. While the days between each breakdown grow fewer and farther between, the experiences are still real and authentic.

This section will give you a glimpse of what mourning may look like. You will be challenged to reflect in ways that are uncomfortable and may trigger different pieces of trauma from your own journey. You will also be reminded that in the midst of your trauma, there is *Hope In The Mourning*. I pray that you feel the Holy Spirit's peace as you journey through this section.

Day 7: Ugly Crying

I feel my eyes swell as I'm choking for air

Snot rolls down my cheek

I'm gasping for hope as my knees buckle

I've never felt this physically weak

Tears begin to pour harder than a storm

My vocal chords shout out in strain!

My mouth quivers as my muscles go numb

A headache rages on from all of this pain

"Don't le-eaveee meee!" I scream

While darkness overpowers me

Judas' kiss rips apart my soul

As the devil continues devouring

satan laughs as my body tightens

I feel another wave coming on

The sun stayed in mourning all of these days

A year without you is far too long

Hope In The Mourning Question: When was the last time you mourned the death of your loved one? What was the experience like? Journal below:

Day 8: Joy Is Behind Me

I faked a smile today. My family needed to see that I was okay, but in all reality I didn't want to wake up to more pain. Probably because I'm an emotional mess without a sense of time.

Please answer me, God, is it night or mourning? Without warning, another wave of depression breaks through. Who knew that this loss would rob me of my joy, making me feel guilty as I enjoy something without them. As if they would want me to.

I don't mean to be rude, God, but where are You? All hope I once had has vanished into the night. I tried going to church again but my fight disappeared along with Your light. *This isn't right.*

I keep fighting back the tears as I try to smile. But a smile weighs more than a mountain. As soon as one appears it evaporates into the abyss. The reality I am facing is that joy is behind me. I don't feel hope anymore, no, hope is gone.

How can I ever be happy again when the person who made me happiest is dead? Instead, I feel broken, discouraged, and alone. Please bring them back home. I want to hear their footsteps slamming across the floors once more.

Hope In The Mourning Question: What was something you and your loved one used to do that brought you the most joy? Have you been able to do that thing since they passed? Journal below:

____

____

____

____

____

____

____

____

____

____

____

____

Day 9: Prayer for Peace

Dear God, I couldn't sleep yesterday. I continued to wake up in puddles of sweat throughout the night. I have experienced fight or flight emotions since my loved one died. I feel like I am in last place while running this race. Mourning continues to hit me in different ways and at a different pace.

Along with this, I ugly-cried last week after I thought I heard their voice in the store. How much more can I endure before I am taken too?

I pray for peace. I pray for Your presence to be noticeable at least. Would You hold me, God? Philippians 4:7 says that You provide a peace that surpasses *all* understanding.

So I here I am, barely standing. I am asking for *that* type of peace. I am asking for You to step in and walk with me while I am weak, in the moments when darkness overwhelms me and I am paralyzed by pain. Please don't forget about me, Father.

Amen.

Hope In The Mourning Prayer: Write out your own "Prayer for Peace" down below:

____

____

____

____

____

____

____

____

____

____

____

____

Day 10: Paralyzed By Pain

Pain paralyzes every part of me

My body feels numb with apathy

The weight of the mourning surpasses gravity

But the duties of the day call me forward

Grogginess asphyxiates my motivation to wake

I look through the window at an anesthetic daybreak

I crawl out of bed as my body aches

Because the day is calling me forward

Hope In The Mourning Question: How difficult is it for you to attend to the day ahead? What are some things you have done in the morning that give you hope for the day? Journal below:

____

____

____

____

____

____

____

____

____

____

____

____

Day 11: Reflection Questions & Reactivate Faith Verse

1) In what ways has your body physically responded to your loss?

2) When experiencing loss outwardly, do you like to be alone or surrounded by people?

Reactivate Faith Verse: *"Then David said to Joab and all the people with him, 'Tear your clothes and put on sackcloth and walk in mourning in front of Abner.' King David himself walked behind the bier. They buried Abner in Hebron, and the king wept aloud at Abner's tomb. All the people wept also. The king sang this lament for Abner: 'Should Abner have died as the lawless die? Your hands were not buried your feet were not fettered. You fell as one falls before the wicked.' And all the people wept over him again." (2 Samuel 3:31-34, NRSV).*

Part 3: The Battle of The Mind

"Just because no one else can heal or do your inner work for you, doesn't mean you can, should, or need to do it alone." - Lisa Olivera

Section Introduction: The Battle Wages On

I was sixteen when I started experiencing panic attacks. I found myself in the middle of the night waking up in puddles of sweat as my body attempted to settle down. Unfortunately, losing my father the following year only intensified the mental health battles I was fighting. Along with anxiety and panic attacks, I began journeying through depression, feelings of worthlessness, and feelings of loneliness. I also began struggling with fears of losing others whom I was close with. The devil was destroying my confidence and will to live by attacking me through my mind.

Mental health is something that not everyone struggles with. Some of you have never had a panic attack nor battled depression after losing a loved one. Others may experience anxiety and depression while also struggling with the fear of loss. Some may be suicidal, while others are battling eating disorders and insecurities.

The point is this: Whether you struggle with mental health or not, I believe this section will be extremely helpful for you as you journey through loss. If you do struggle with mental health, I pray that you are able to relate to the words and find hope in between the lines. If you do not struggle with mental health issues, I believe you will be better equipped to walk with those who do after reading some of the things people experience.

I invite you to jump right in to this section with an open heart and settled mind. In order to do this, pray for a conscious spirit.

Day 12: Breastplate of Anxiety

My heart feels oppressed by the weight that covers me
A simple sound makes me shiver
My heart is always in a dance with its beat
God, where are You now?
I'm gasping for breath, but fear constantly strangles me
Reminding me of my stress and telling me of what's yet to be
This fear of loss thing is really starting to mess with me
Hold on honey, let me tell you for the fifth time to please drive safely
There she leaves to do the things she does daily
Now I believe in the power of prayer,
But it's hard to pray when my mind won't slow down
God, help me see in the darkness that's surrounding me
Help me hope in the chaos that's overwhelming me
Help me feel life again without having to breathe so heavily
I want to be able to wake up with a heartbeat beating steadily
If You're listening God, please just hold me
I'd do anything to feel Your power,
Instead of the power that's been controlling me
I'd do anything to live life again without fear taking over me
Please help me out with this battle that I am in
Please be my guidance as I'm battling within
I'm overwhelmed as I walk towards the gate
God please help me take off this breastplate of anxiety

Hope In The Mourning Question: Since you have lost your loved one, have you experienced the fear of loss? Has this fear caused anxiety for you? Journal below:

____

____

____

____

____

____

____

____

____

____

____

____

Day 13: Fight or Flight

Breath escapes me as I prepare for battle
The war in my brain wages on
My mind is locked and loaded with ammunition
I feel control slipping away

I have not prepared for this
I couldn't have prepared for this
Yet here I stand armed and dangerous
Feeling control slip away

The first shot sounds and I buckle in fear
Panic covers my body
Blood begins to drench my forehead
My arms begin to shake

I force myself to safety
Today was not a good day
Crawling back into bed I go
While control is slipping away

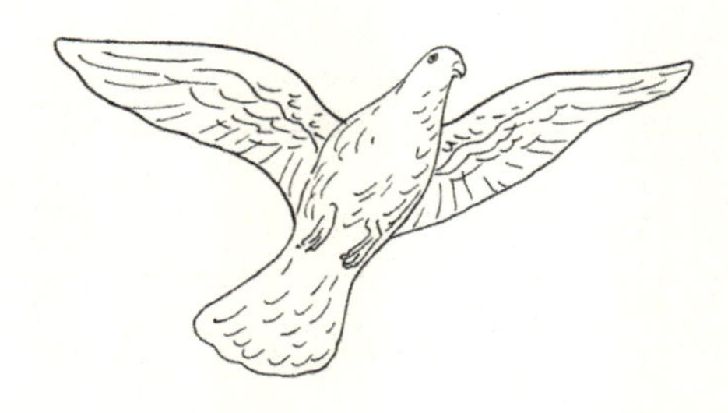

Hope In The Mourning Question: Have you ever felt like you were in a fight-or-flight experience? What was that situation like for you? Journal below:

____

____

____

____

____

____

____

____

____

____

____

____

Day 14: Prayer for Strength

Dear God, I am weak. I seek to know Your strength. I cannot do this without You. My mind is racing with fear. I always feel alone and I am desperate for You to be near. I am terrified that I will lose another loved one. I am breathless as I begin to grasp the weight of my grief. All of these dreams I'm having are causing me to lose sleep. *What do they mean?*

Please give me strength in the moments when I feel weakest. Please provide me with a sense of hope when I am feeling conquered by fatigue. You are the only hope I need. And while I believe that You are still with me, I need help overcoming my unbelief. Help me see through the darkness that is surrounding me. Help me feel Your power when I am completely broken.

I believe that You are capable of moving mountains. I pray that You surround me with the same power. I pray that You give me strength when my fight-or-flight instincts kick in. I pray that You fill me with joy when I am overpowered by pain. You are the only strength that has remained.

Amen

Hope In The Mourning Question: Write out your own "Prayer for Strength" below:

____

____

____

____

____

____

____

____

____

____

____

____

Day 15: Deep In Depression

I am used to sadness now
Its darkness provides comfort I willingly allow

Its grip leads me to despair
Gravitating towards hope, I ache for repair

Some days I feel hope breaking through
Like a tool twisting in a rusty screw

Other moments I am stuck in a maze
Choking on lies and shame

Is this what depression feels like?

Hope In The Mourning Question: Depression can be suffocating. Have you experienced depression or deep sadness since you lost your loved one? What has that been like for you? Journal below:

Day 16: Surviving Saturday

Pain
What is pain?
What is the point of these feelings that won't go away?
What is the antidote for these emotions on this Saturday?
Sometimes my strength is stripped from me without warning
Sometimes my insecurities are weighing me down
I cry in a corner and shiver because of every lie I'm fighting
I'm dealing with anxiety and feelings of worthlessness,
Can anyone else relate?
I try to leave them behind when God says go,
But I am tempted to hang around because the devil says…
Stay.
And so stay I must
Because I am perverted with fear
How ironic that the very things that should bring joy,
Are the things that rock my faith
God, I don't like feeling this way
Right now, I'm waiting for the resurrection
While trying to survive on Saturday

Hope In The Mourning Question: After Jesus was crucified, the Disciples and followers of Jesus spent Saturday feeling completely hopeless. Little did they know that the resurrection of Christ was right around the corner. Do you find yourself feeling hopeless on *Saturday*? Journal below:

____

____

____

____

____

____

____

____

____

____

____

Day 17: Gentle Whisper

Father, in the midst of all of my suffering, my soul is buffering and clinging on to You. It's true that You are my only refuge. In the midst of this journey, I have experienced every type of emotion… but I guess that is the reality of grief. One day I am cursing You out while the next day I am clinging on to hope that only You can provide. *Please, never leave my side*.

While I am struggling with despair and strife, I cling to Your light. I cling to the Truth that You are in control. There is no other way. In the midst of my anxiety and pain, I am reminded that You were slain for me. Grief is a journey that reminds me of the sacrificial Majesty. So while I am continuing to mourn and grieve my loved one, I lean in and listen to Your gentle whisper.

Hope In The Mourning Question: Has it been difficult for you to remember God's promises since you lost your loved one? In what ways has your loss hurt and helped your faith? Journal below:

____

____

____

____

____

____

____

____

____

____

____

____

Day 18: Reflection Questions & Reactivate Faith Verse

1) Do you battle any form of mental illness? If so, list below

2) How has mental illness affected you or your loved ones since your loss?

3) What are aome things you or your loved ones do to combat mental illness?

Reactivate Faith Verse: *"Do not be anxious about anything, but in every situation, by prayer and petition, with thanksgiving, present your requests to God. And the peace of God, which transcends all understanding, will guard your hearts and your minds in Christ Jesus" (Philippians 4:6-7, NIV).*

Part 4: Grief

"No one ever told me that grief felt so like fear." - C.S. Lewis, *A Grief Observed*

Section Introduction: The Never-ending Journey

Sometimes we underestimate how traumatic the grieving process can be. I find myself looking at the Psalms and watching how David grieved throughout each chapter. Some chapters he is filled with hope, joy, praise, and worship, while in others he is crying out to God mourning the death of his child.

The problem with grief is that none of us are truly experts on it. Those who have experienced loss certainly have more insight on how to grieve in a healthier way, but one thing must be made clear: Grief affects each and every one of us differently. Our response towards loss is unique to *our journey.*

There may be days when you are feeling like you could climb a mountain, and other days when the valley has become your home. But guess what? God meets us in the tension between the two locations and holds us while we grieve.

You may be wondering, "Isn't this entire devotional about grieving?" Yes, it is. However, I wanted to include a section specific to the theme of grief because *grieving never truly ends*.

While mourning will slow down and mental health can become manageable, grieving will be a part of our journey for the rest of our lives. We must not hide from this part of the journey once the *new normal* has become a reality for us.

During this section, I invite you to start focusing on how your relationship with God has been impacted since your loss. When reality finally sinks in that our lives will never go back to "the way things were," what does that leave you with in terms of how you view God?

Grieving has the ability to increase the *realness* and *authenticity* of our relationship with Jesus. But it also has the ability to tear it down.

This section will give you opportunities to grieve with God. Different questions and prompts will challenge you to confront God head-on with your loss. Because remember, it is in the tension between the mountain and the valley that I believe God holds us.

Day 19: Grief Feels Like

Grief feels like weak legs and a stomachache

Grief feels like being stabbed in the chest

Grief feels like a panic attack that never fully goes away

Grief feels like a broken bone that never fully heals

Grief feels like unhealthy weight loss and weight gain

Grief feels like breath that weighs one hundred pounds

Grief feels like bland food and unbrushed teeth

Grief feels like an unclean house

Grief feels like jet lag

Grief feels like sleepless nights

Grief feels like grapes being crushed for wine

Grief feels like being trapped in space while gravity still holds you down

Grief feels like someone cutting one thousand slivers into my skin, yet the scars appear on my heart

Grief feels like hope trying to make sense of chaos

Grief feels like sadness escaping its prison

Grief feels like hell

Hope In The Mourning Question: What does grief feel like for you? Journal below:

____

____

____

____

____

____

____

____

____

____

____

____

Day 20: The Weight of Hope

Hope feels heavy
Weighing me down as I seek it
Pressing me on every side
Calling me forward at too fast a pace

Hope feels far
The distance too long to journey
Sweat forms at my heart as I chase it
The journey is exhausting

Hope feels silent
Dreams don't shout like my aching heart does
Pain pulses through my eardrums
The road is far from over

Hope feels necessary
Without it my body breaks
Like a morning without coffee,
I need hope to survive

The weight of hope just might be worth it

Hope In The Mourning Question: In what things do you place your hope? Journal below:

___

___

___

___

___

___

___

___

___

___

___

___

Day 21: Letter To God

Dear God,
I am Broken
I am painfully putting together the pieces of my past that spell hopeless
I am shattered beyond any strength that could realign my focus
I am absolutely broken
How could anyone look at me in love?
How can you believe that my existence is enough?
My baggage weighs me down like an anchor
Every breath feels like facing a gladiator in the Colosseum
Pointless.
Who am I to believe that you still look at me with grace?
Let's face it, God, I was a creator's mistake
If you are there, God, why can't I feel you?
If you still believe in me, God, show me some real proof
Because right now, I feel abandoned
Signed,
"Your Child."

Dear Child,
Why do you define yourself by your brokenness?
Why do you pursue fear rather than love?
When will you come home?
I am broken every moment that you feel alone
I did not die for you so that you would carry this on your own
I know that you feel abandoned and shattered
Believe me when I say that I created you with a purpose,
You truly do matter
I know that your grief feels heavy, so did my cross
Don't devalue my resurrection by running away lonely and lost
Truth be told, I would die again even if you were the only one it would save
Truth be told, you were not then, are not now, a mistake
Take those quotations off of your name, and believe that you are My Child
Not a moment goes by that you are not worth My while
In your darkest grief, don't run away, run nearer to Me
Regardless of your past mistakes, I will always love you
Signed,
Your Biggest Fan

Hope In The Mourning Question: If you could write a letter to God, what would it say? Journal below:

____

____

____

____

____

____

____

____

____

____

____

____

Day 22: Prayer for Patience

God, my soul is restless. I feel like I am being tested and my patience is running out. How long will it take for You to show me the goodness that is supposed to be woven throughout Your plan?

I pray for patience as you hold my hand in the presence of my grief. Even though I don't understand what You are doing, I will quiet my heart and trust in You. Break through the barriers that are suffocating my chest. Give me rest.

Lord, I see in Hebrews chapter 11 that Your strongest warriors didn't see the end result of their faith. That scares me a little bit as I try to concentrate on Your purpose for me. Be with me as I grieve. Please don't ever leave. Give me patience in the moments when my soul is chasing answers to things. Give me patience while my heart is overwhelmed with anxiety. Give me patience even when I have no desire to wait patiently.

I love You, God.

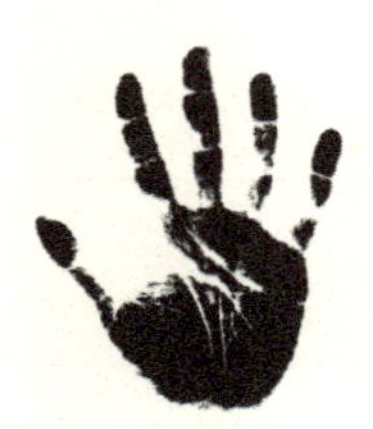

Hope In The Mourning Question: Write out your own "Prayer for Patience" below:

Day 23: The Garden of Grief

I sit here on my knees in the garden of grief
Where does my hope come from?
The mourning is exposing my every need
What else might God have done?

The enemy's voice is loud as blood drips from my brow
My hands begin to shake
The other path exposes the darker route
God, is there another way?

I walk over to my support and find them asleep
I need their prayers
A text message of encouragement would work just fine
Slowly they're turning into my betrayers

This garden is holistically overwhelming me
I feel hope clashing with pain
This journey is about surrendering my will for Yours
So hold me while I pray

Hope In The Mourning Question: Have you ever asked God why He allows bad things to happen? What has His answer been? Journal below:

____

____

____

____

____

____

____

____

____

____

____

____

Day 24: Reflection Questions & Reactivate Faith Verse

1) In what ways have you felt grief show up in your life throughout the journey?

2) What days or holidays have been the hardest to live through since your loss?

3) What do you miss most about your loved one?

Reactivate Faith Verse: *"I have told you these things, so that in me you may have peace. In this world you will have trouble. But take heart! I have overcome the world" (John 16:33, NIV).*

Part 5: Hope In The Mourning

"God gave us memory so that we might have roses in December." - J.M. Barrie, *Courage*

Section Introduction: Hope Within

If we're being honest with ourselves, hope is such a difficult concept for us to fully understand. For those of us who believe in an afterlife, how do we have faith that whatever comes after this will be better than our suffering? Sin and suffering have distorted our image of the truth that *it will be better than this*.

We beg God for it to be better than *this*, now. Yet, that's not how God works. Our faith reminds us that suffering is a part of everyone's journey. But our mind convinces us that we can live a full life without experiencing such suffering. We cling to what is *easy* rather than what is *good*.

C.S. Lewis is known for his belief that God isn't safe, but good. I resonate with that.

My hope for you while journeying through this section is that in the midst of your mourning and grieving, you too can feel the goodness of God. Sometimes this may come in the form of peace while the storm is surrounding you. Sometimes this may come in a generous act of a stranger when your body is aching for joy. Whatever this section brings you, my ultimate hope is this: You understand that you aren't always going to feel *this* way.

Yes there will be tears, body aches, anxiety, depression, fears, guilt, shame, sin, and suffering along the way. *But there is hope in the mourning*. Paul addresses this concept while writing a letter to the church in Rome. He writes one of my favorite verses in the entire Bible in this letter:

* * *

*"**For I am convinced** that neither death, nor life, nor angels, nor rulers, nor things present, nor things to come, nor powers, nor height, nor depth, nor anything else in all creation, will be able to separate us from the love of God in Christ Jesus our Lord" (Romans 8:38-39, NRSV, emphasis my own).*

Paul was arrested at least three times. He was stoned to death and somehow survived (see Acts 14). He was beaten and mocked, all for the sake of the glory of the Kingdom of God. In the presence of all of this suffering, he chose to be convinced that there is only one King that will satisfy his aching soul.

He chooses to seek *Hope in the Mourning*. My prayer for you is that you would choose the same.

Day 25: God Is Not Done Yet

My soul rejoices as my heart aches
Suffering is real, but so is faith
The pain is not gone, but neither is my strength
This journey has reminded me that death will break
So here I stand in the journey
Hopefully sitting in sorrow
Waiting for a better tomorrow, I trust in Christ alone
God has shown me through the thick and thin,
That within my soul there is ***victory***
While I'm aching from loss and clinging to hope
This truth remains: abandonment and God are contradictory
I am strong
I am hopeful
I believe that God is not done yet

Hope In The Mourning Question: As you journey through loss, you will have days of hope and days of pain. However, if you are still breathing, I believe God is not done with you yet. In what ways can God use your grief for His Kingdom? Journal below:

____

____

____

____

____

____

____

____

____

____

____

Day 26: Evidence of Victory

One breath at at time, I see victory
It comes in brief moments covered by tears, but it's there
Its strength holds me as I kneel
Its love welcomes me as I scream

Loss is not the equivalent of defeat
As one chapter closes, God continues the story
Slowly but surely hope covers the pages
Slowly but surely, victory breaks through

It may not be during my lifetime, or even the next
I may not see the final impact
Yet I trust that God is going to use this for good
God always does

There is evidence of victory breaking through the shadows
I will not let the enemy have the last laugh
I will use this loss for God's Kingdom
I will not be shaken

For God is my refuge and my strength
God is the Alpha and the Omega, beginning and end
God is the King of all Kings and the One who holds me
God is Victory

Hope In The Mourning Question: What are a few blessings—no matter how small—that have come from your loss? Journal below:

____

____

____

____

____

____

____

____

____

____

____

____

Day 27: Prayer of Praise

God, I thank You for this journey. I thank You for the mourning and storming in of Your presence. While I haven't felt it every day, I feel Your love in this moment. Clothed in sadness, I feel Your arms holding me.

I miss my loved one more than words have meaning for. I miss the way they would hug me, hold me, laugh with me, and scold me.

I miss the way they supported me in times of discouragement. I seek your encouragement, Father, and praise You for the time I *did* have with them. While it was not enough, You taught me how to appreciate the times I have with everyone. You've called me deeper into a relationship with You because of this loss.

I still don't understand why they died… but I think that's okay. My faith is shaken but I'm leaning in to Your grace, love, and praise. You are my source of strength. You hold me when I am weak and comfort me when I feel alone. I feel at home when I am leaning into Your presence.

Amen.

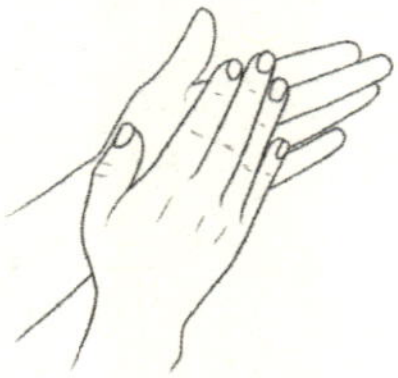

Hope In The Mourning Question: As difficult as it may be, I encourage you to write out your own "Prayer of Praise" below:

____

____

____

____

____

____

____

____

____

____

____

____

Day 28: I Still Miss You, And That's Okay

I still miss you, but I think that's okay. Though the skies remain gray I see hope through the window frame. My life has carried on along with my pain, but in the middle of the chaos I have invited God into this space.

And so here I am, sitting in this holistic tension. Trying to give God my full attention while my heart is being pulled in different directions. In the midst of this spiritual dissension, I find peace, knowing that God does not judge me for wrestling.

For the truth of the matter is, my life will never be the same. A piece of me is missing and while this grief can be tamed, it cannot be completely erased. Their memory is stitched and forever engraved in my heart. So even if I break down in Walmart, I trust that God will hold me in the moments of despair.

I still miss you, and that's okay.

Hope In The Mourning Question: Have you ever been pressured to "move on" from your loss? What was that experience like? How did it make you feel? Journal below:

____

____

____

____

____

____

____

____

____

____

____

____

Day 29: Hope In The Mourning

I get ready for bed, tucked in by fear and despair
I try to fall asleep wondering if anyone is there
My heart feels suppressed by the things deemed unfair
Yet this darkness won't be the victor

How many times must I shout and scream,
Before light abolishes the pain and death loses its sting?
How many times must my lungs stretch out to breathe,
Before darkness fades a little bit quicker?

I feel overwhelmed by the night, but try to hold on
Falling asleep is my safe haven while I long for the dawn
I will stand my ground watching demons spawn
But fighting this darkness is making me sicker

There it is, the light is steadily rising
A new day is coming, a day I'll be fighting
Joy bursts through and though the darkness is enticing
I know that I can find hope in the mourning

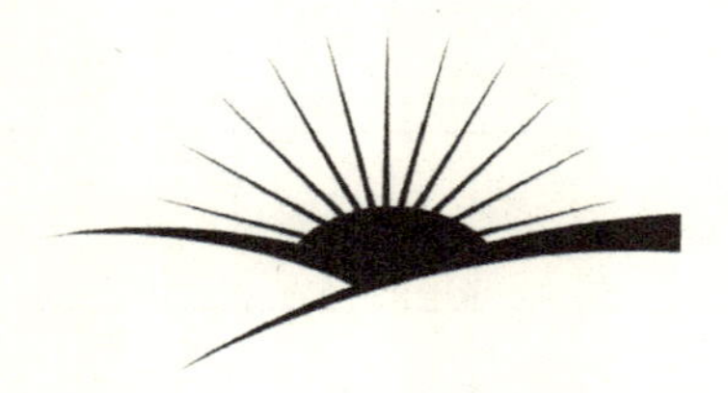

Hope In The Mourning Question: Is it difficult for you to lean into the concept of hope? If so, why is that? If not, what helps you? Journal below:

____

____

____

____

____

____

____

____

____

____

____

____

Day 30: Reflection Questions & Reactivate Faith Verse

1) What evidence of God's presence have you seen since your loss?

2) What do you look forward to most about Heaven?

Reactivate Faith Verse: *"For his anger lasts only a moment, but his favor lasts a lifetime; weeping may stay for the night, but rejoicing comes in the morning" (Psalms 30:5, NIV).*

Conclusion: The Problem of Pain

My heart was not designed to carry this much grief.

After reading C.S. Lewis' famous work *The Problem of Pain*, I began processing why pain hurts so badly. If you've experienced any form of suffering, you know that pain feels like your body is suffocating even though your lungs continue to function properly. Your heart is heavy and filled with grief as you begin to wrestle with the new normal—the new journey you have been forced to endure.

So, what is the problem of pain? *Why do pain and suffering and grief make you feel like your world is falling apart?*

When we read the Creation story in Genesis, we see that everything God created was good. God separated the light from the dark, the sky from the ground, and everything His paintbrush painted was *good*. Then sin happened and it distorted the beautiful image God painted. Sin catacombs everything God created, giving humans this choice: God's original design or humanity's manmade painting.

We can choose to endure the suffering—as painful as it is—and lean in to the painting God has designed us for, or we can choose a life of selfishness and simplicity by pursuing the things the world encourages us to chase after. Because we choose sin every single day, our bodies continue to deteriorate.

After journeying through the loss of my father for seven years, I came to this conclusion:

The problem with pain is that our bodies were not designed to experience it. Our bodies were designed to experience love.

When God created you, He created you to experience the goodness of His plan and the fulfillment of His promises. He created you to experience love and *love alone*. Suffering hurts because it goes against God's original design.

So if suffering wasn't the original plan, why does God allow it? Why did God allow my daddy to die? Why did God allow your child to die? Why does cancer exist and why has COVID-19 taken the lives of millions of people worldwide? Let me draw your attention back to God's original painting for our lives:

1) Everything God created was declared ***good.***

2) We were created to experience ***love.***

You're right. God could just as easily snap His fingers and eliminate suffering as He used His paintbrush to create the world. Yet, pain provides us with the opportunity to understand the fullness of God's goodness and experience the wholeness of God's love for us. Here's what I mean: Humanity chose sin to fulfill its desires yet God chose suffering to fulfill His. Paul writes that even though we are still sinners, God sent His son Jesus to experience the suffering of the world for each and every one of us through death on a cross (see Romans 5:8).

God's original plan was postponed, but it wasn't erased. Because of this, here is the Truth: Your suffering can be used for **good** and for **love**, but you have to choose it. Each and every day you wake up, you have the opportunity to choose to use your tragedy for triumph and then watch God work.

This is much easier said than don. It took me seven years of journeying through grief to get to this place. I used to say that I would do *anything* to have my dad back in my life. I used to beg God each and every day to raise my daddy from the dead so that I could have him back in my life. Now I am begging God each and every day to keep my daddy away from this sinful place so that I can continue to use my pain for His purposes.

Don't get me wrong. I still miss my dad each and every single day, but there are people in this world who God has created me to help find hope. Without my story of loss, I wouldn't have the platform to do so. God is using my loss to ensure that everything He created draws near to His ***goodness*** and experiences the fullness of His ***love.***

If my suffering can help hurting people find *Hope In The Mourning*, **then I will gladly suffer.**

I want to close by saying this: There is nothing you could ever go through that you will go through alone. Even after Adam and Eve chose a life of sin after God created the world, *God was still with them.* Even after the Israelites continued to do evil in the eyes of the Lord throughout the entirety of the Old Testament, *God was still with them.* Even after His own people nailed Him and crucified Him on a tree, *God was still with them.*

How do I know this? *Because Jesus came back.* I'm not talking about the Resurrection. Jesus could have resurrected and then reappeared in a different part of the world if He wanted to. But He chose to come back and reappear to the very people who had beaten Him, mocked Him, and killed Him. Why?

Because Jesus knew that His suffering would bring hope to those who were lost. Jesus knew that the enemy wouldn't be able to survive after they saw the ***goodness*** of God's promises and the fullness of God's ***love*** come back to fruition—come back to the very situation that had caused Him so much pain and choose to use it to complete His promises. This choice alone would then provide hope, healing, goodness, and love for the rest of humanity.

You can choose this too.

About the Author

Jordan Daniel Chitwood is a Jesus follower with a vision to carry on the revolution that Jesus started. He has a wife named Marissa, a son named Uriah, and an Australian Kelpie named Theo. Jordan is the Online Pastor and a Teaching Pastor at Crossbridge Community Church with a passion to help hurting people find hope. He likes to read, write, listen to music, play video games, and hang out with friends in his free time. In the midst of his pain, Jordan believes God is with him every single step of the way. One step at a time, God is molding Jordan into the man God created him to be.

Stay Connected:

Website: www.jordandanielchitwood.com

Instagram: jordandanielchitwood

Twitter: Jordan_Chitwood

Facebook: JordanDanielChitwood

Blog: www.jordandanielchitwood.com/blog

Made in United States
North Haven, CT
06 March 2023